10/12

Black History Makers

Musicians

Debbie Foy

PowerKiDS press.

New York

Published in 2012 by The Rosen Publishing Group, Inc.
29 East 21st Street, New York, NY 10010

Editor: Katie Woolley, Jennifer Way
Designer: Tim Mayer, MayerMedia
Consultant: Mia Morris, Black History Month Web Site

Picture Acknowledgments: Cover, p. 15 Jeff Albertson/Corbis; Title page, pp. 12, 16, 20, 21, 22 (bottom right) Shutterstock; pp. 3, 11 David Corio/Michael Ochs Archives/Getty Images; pp. 4, 6 Bettmann/Corbis; p. 5 James L. Amos/Corbis; p. 7 Pictorial Press/Alamy; p. 8 William Gottlieb/Redferns/Getty Images; p. 9 Sasha/Getty; p. 10 Tim Mosenfelder/Getty Imagers; p. 13 Gareth Cattermole/Getty Images; pp. 14, 18, 22 (bottom left), 22 (top center), 22 (top left) Michael Ochs Archives/Corbis; p. 17 Joey Foley/FilmMagic/Getty Images; pp. 18–19 Georges de Keerle/Getty Images; p. 22 (top right) Nils Jorgensen/Rex Features; p. 22 (bottom center) Douglas Kent Hall/ZUMA/Corbis.

Library of Congress Cataloging-in-Publication Data

Foy, Debbie.
Musicians / by Debbie Foy. — 1st ed.
    p. cm. — (Black history makers)
Includes index.
ISBN 978-1-4488-6637-3 (library binding) — ISBN 978-1-4488-7052-3 (pbk.) — ISBN 978-1-4488-7053-0 (6-pack)
1. Musicians, Black—Biography—Juvenile literature. I. Title.
ML3929.F69 2012
780.92'396—dc23
[B]
                    2011029713

Manufactured in Malaysia

WEB SITES:

Due to the changing nature of Internet links, PowerKids Press has developed an online list of Web sites related to the subject of this book. This site is updated regularly. Please use this link to access the list:
powerkidslinks.com/blackhist/music/

CPSIA Compliance Information: Batch #WW2102PK: For Further Information contact Rosen Publishing, New York, New York at 1-800-237-9932

CONTENTS

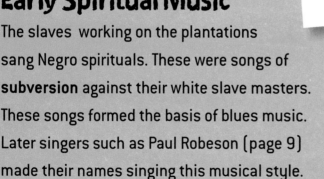

What Is Black Music?

In the seventeenth century, millions of African people were sent around the world to work as slaves. Many were shipped to the American colonies to be slaves on the cotton **plantations**. They brought with them songs and music styles from hundreds of ethnic groups across West Africa. These musical forms blended with other European influences and continued to change throughout the eighteenth and nineteenth centuries to form black music as we know it today.

When black people were transported from Africa to be slaves, they brought with them songs from many ethnic groups.

Early Spiritual Music

The slaves working on the plantations sang Negro spirituals. These were songs of **subversion** against their white slave masters. These songs formed the basis of blues music. Later singers such as Paul Robeson (page 9) made their names singing this musical style.

The Birth of Jazz

Between the 1890s and the 1920s, a style of music called jazz developed. It was created by African Americans in the southern states of Louisiana, Texas, and Missouri, among others.

Men such as Louis Armstrong (page 8) performed in large orchestra bands and because **segregation** was still in force, they often played to white-only audiences.

The 1950s and 1960s

During these decades, soul and **R&B** became popular styles, with singers like Shirley Bassey (page 12) becoming a legendary soul diva. Funk, said to have been invented by James Brown (page 10), was a blend of many music styles, including jazz and R&B.

The 1970s

The 1970s saw the invention of hip hop. Hip hop grew out of Harlem block parties, which were large public parties held in that neighborhood. Disc jockeys (DJs) spun records, usually funk, while masters of ceremonies (MCs) began improvising lyrics or raps. This musical style gave rise to talents such as Jazzie B (page 22) and later Jay-Z (page 20) and Alicia Keys (page 22). At the same time, **reggae** became a musical force and a focus of **black consciousness**, thanks to artists such as Bob Marley (page 14).

Harlem block parties of the 1970s were usually large, outdoor community gatherings, from which hip hop music emerged.

Pop and Crossover

In the 1980s and 1990s, African American pop and R&B artists such as Michael Jackson (page 18) and Beyoncé (page 21) sang a type of pop dance-soul that became popular. These pop **crossover** success stories paved the way for many other artists, both black and white.

Over four centuries, the music of African Americans has largely dominated the musical landscape. Black music has grown out of slavery, poverty, struggle, and religious belief. In this book we explore how the diverse musical styles of today have been influenced by the legendary black musical history makers of the past.

Louis Armstrong
Founding Father of Jazz

Louis Armstrong's pioneering musical style had an impact on millions of future musicians.

Name: Louis Daniel Armstrong

Born: August 4, 1901, New Orleans, Louisiana

Died: July 6, 1971

Musical talents: Jazz trumpet, cornet, and singing

Interesting fact: The Federal Bureau of Investigation (FBI) kept a file on Louis regarding his outspoken views on **racial integration**.

Born into a poor Louisiana family, Louis Armstrong grew up in the care of his mother and grandmother, rarely seeing his father. From the age of seven, he worked various jobs to help his family financially. One of those jobs was carrying coal to the entertainment district of New Orleans, where he would stand outside the dance halls and listen to the bands playing inside.

On the Mississippi

Armstrong grew up singing in the streets for money and playing the cornet in local bands. In his early twenties, Armstrong also worked the riverboats of New Orleans on the Mississippi River.

He was one of the first jazz players to play trumpet solos and combine singing and **scatting** in his performances.

Speaking Out

Armstrong had strong views on racial integration, some of which were explored in songs, such as "(What Did I Do to Be So) Black and Blue?" During the Little Rock Crisis of 1957, in which the government prevented nine black students from entering the all-white Little Rock High School, Armstrong cancelled a U.S. government-sponsored tour, saying, "The way the government is treating my people in the South, they can go to Hell!"

Louis Armstrong died of a heart attack at the age of 69, but his pioneering musical style and strongly held views on racial integration have had an impact on millions of people.

Paul Robeson
Singer, Actor, and Activist

Early Years

Paul Robeson was the youngst of five children in the Robeson family. At the age of six, Paul's mother died in a house fire and his father lost his job, so the family relocated to Somerville, New Jersey.

Great Talent

At his new school, Robeson was talented in the classroom, onstage, and on the sports field. Robeson graduated from college with good grades and moved to New York to study law. He worked as a lawyer while singing and acting in his free time.

Spreading the Word

In 1928, Robeson starred in a London production of the musical *Show Boat* and his career took off. In spite of his popularity, Robeson had to deal with racism. From the mid-1940s onward, he devoted himself to political causes.

In 1949, Robeson toured Europe to speak out against the **discrimination** against black Americans. After some of his appearances ended in riots the United States government refused to allow him to travel abroad, so he toured the United States encouraging black people to fight for their rights.

Charismatic Man

Paul Robeson was an outspoken man who used his position in the limelight to fight injustice and try to bring about social change.

Name: Paul Leroy Robeson

Born: April 9, 1898, Princeton, New Jersey

Died: January 23, 1976

Musical talent: Singing

Interesting fact: Paul sent his nine-year-old son to school in the Soviet Union to avoid the racism Paul had suffered at school.

Paul Robeson was an athlete, actor, singer, academic, author, and political activist.

James Brown
The Godfather of Soul

James was known as "the hardest working man in show business" because of his drive and limitless energy.

Name: James Joseph Brown

Born: May 3, 1933, Barnwell, South Carolina

Died: December 25, 2006

Musical talent: Singing, songwriting, keyboards, and guitar

Interesting fact: As a young child, James was so poor that one day his school sent him home for having "insufficient clothes." This may explain why in later life James loved to dress elaborately.

Early Influences

James Brown's parents divorced when he was five, so he was raised mainly by his great-aunt. Growing up during the **Great Depression** of the 1930s and in the segregated Southern states, Brown faced extreme poverty and racial discrimination. He learned to play the drums and guitar and was influenced by watching gospel preachers scream, dance, and fall to their knees during sermons.

First Recording

At the age of 15, Brown was arrested for breaking into cars and ended up at reform school, where he formed a gospel group. He later joined an R&B band called The Famous Flames and, in 1956, they produced their first recording "Please, Please, Please." The track sold more than one million copies and launched Brown's musical career.

The 1960s and 1970s

In the 1960s, Brown's music was often associated with black **nationalist** movements and tracks such as "Say It Loud – I'm Black and Proud"

James Brown was known for his exciting stage shows that were feats of timing and great energy!

(1968) were seen as a civil rights anthem.

In the 1970s, his songs featured on the sound tracks for the popular **blaxploitation** films *Black Caesar* (1973) and *Slaughter's Big Rip-Off* (1973).

The Later Years

When hip hop emerged in the 1980s, DJs and songwriters frequently sampled Brown's songs on their tracks and James Brown continued to be known by a new generation as the "Godfather of Soul."

Brown had many setbacks in his life, including the death of his wife, legal troubles, drug use, and poor health. He died at the age of 73. His elaborate memorial service involved a bronze casket and videos of his concert performances.

MAKING HISTORY

James Brown was one of the most influential figures in twentieth century music. Renowned for his vocal screams, his feverish dance moves, and his extravagant sense of style, James Brown put the notion of rhythm on the pop musical map and played a major part in the development of soul and funk.

Shirley Bassey
The Original "Bond Girl"

Bassey's big voice and love of glamorous clothes and jewelry identifies her as a performer who loves to put on a show!

Name: Dame Shirley Veronica Bassey

Born: January 8, 1937, Cardiff, Wales, United Kingdom

Musical talents: Singing

Interesting fact: Shirley Bassey is often affectionately nicknamed Burly Chassis, in reference to her powerful voice and lungs.

In October 1964, Bassey topped the charts in the UK and US with "Goldfinger," the theme to the James Bond film of the same name. She followed with several other hits in the 1960s, including the enormously successful "Big Spender" (1967).

James Bond

"Goldfinger" led to two further Bond theme collaborations: "Diamonds Are Forever" (1972) and "Moonraker" (1979). During the 1980s, she fell out of the public eye but in 1997, just before her sixtieth birthday, she came back with a collaboration on a new album with the band Propellerheads. The album, called *History Repeating*, attracted a whole new generation of dance fans and brought Bassey back into the limelight.

Beginnings

Shirley Bassey was the seventh child of Nigerian parents. She left school at the age of 15 to work in a factory and sang in bars and clubs in the evenings and on weekends. She was discovered by a bandleader, Jack Hylton, and in 1955, she left Cardiff for the bright lights of London. Just two years later, Bassey had a top 10 hit with her first single, "The Banana Boat Song" (1957).

Later Success

Bassey's reign as the Welsh diva of the music industry has lasted for five decades. With a love of glamour and her trademark powerful voice, she has enjoyed one of the longest chart careers in British history. To top a distinguished career in showbusiness, the United Kingdom honored Bassey with the title of Dame in 2000!

Dame Shirley Bassey wowed the audience at the BBC's Electric Proms festival in 2009.

Bob Marley
Reggae Hero

Name: Robert (Bob) Nesta Marley

Born: February 6, 1945, Nine Mile, Jamaica

Died: May 11, 1981

Musical talent: Singing and songwriting of reggae and **ska** music

Interesting fact: His song lyrics are often highly political, including the words of Haile Selassie, the twentieth century Ethiopian emperor and key figure in the **Rastafari** movement.

Through his music Bob Marley helped to spread the word of the Rastafari movement to a worldwide audience.

Rural Childhood

The son of a black teenage mother and an older, white father, Marley spent his childhood growing up in a village in Jamaica. With his friend Bunny Livingston (later known as Bunny Wailer), he learned the guitar and practiced his singing skills.

Big Break

In the late 1950s, he moved to Kingston, Jamaica, living in one of the poorest areas of the city. Marley and Livingston formed a band called the Wailing Wailers in the 1960s. While they had some success in Jamaica, the band found it difficult to make money. In 1972, however, they landed a record contract and success soon followed.

In 1974, a track from their *Burnin'* album entitled "I Shot the Sheriff" was covered by Eric Clapton. It became a number one hit in the United States, putting the renamed Bob Marley & The Wailers on the musical map.

Reggae Superstar

The band toured the world, spreading the word on reggae. In the United Kingdom, they had their first top 40 hit with "No Woman, No Cry" (1975).

During the late 1970s, Marley became an international music superstar. His fame and nationalist beliefs made him a target for people who were opposed to his ideas however. After a failed **assassination** attempt in Jamaica in 1976, Marley fled to London.

Last Years

The band traveled to Africa and played at the independence ceremony for Zimbabwe in 1980. They had planned a tour of the United States to promote the album *Uprising* (1980) but were stopped when Marley became ill with cancer. Just before his death at the age of 36, he received the Order of Merit from the Jamaican government. Adored by Jamaicans, he was given a hero's burial.

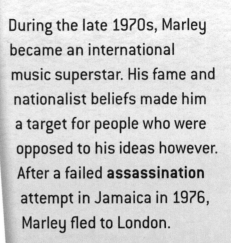

Bob Marley is often remembered for his protest songs in support of social revolution, but he also released many gentle, soothing love songs.

MAKING HISTORY

Bob Marley is credited with being the world ambassador for reggae and a key figure in the Rastafari, or rasta, movement. This movement drew its beliefs from many sources. He was also one of the first international superstars to come from a so-called developing country.

66 I don't stand for the black man's side. I don't stand for the white man's side. I stand for God's side. 99

Bob Marley

Stevie Wonder
The Singer with a Vision

Stevie Wonder was born six weeks early and was blind from birth. Nevertheless, his parents were determined Stevie would live a normal childhood. They encouraged his love of music from an early age. He was a member of the church choir and played a number of instruments including the piano, harmonica, drums, and bass.

First Recording

At just 11 years old, the talented youngster impressed Berry Gordy, the owner of Motown Records in Detroit. Motown was the highest-profile black-owned record label in America. As Little Stevie Wonder, Wonder released two albums in 1962. He had a number one hit in the US pop and R&B charts with a song called "Fingertips (Pt. 2)" in 1963.

Social Activist

Wonder's music had a lot in common with the civil rights movement's desire for integration and for a better deal for working-class African Americans. His classic recordings from the late 1960s through the late 1970s such as "Living for the City" (1973) dealt with poverty and racial tension. The number one single "You Haven't Done Nothin'" (1974) was a protest song against the disgraced president Richard Nixon, who was forced to resign over the **Watergate Scandal** in 1974.

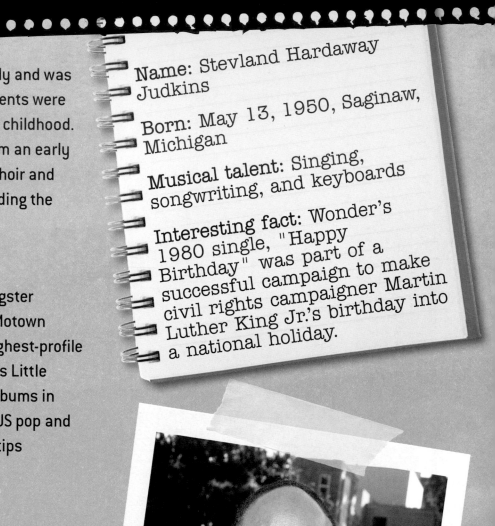

Name: Stevland Hardaway Judkins

Born: May 13, 1950, Saginaw, Michigan

Musical talent: Singing, songwriting, and keyboards

Interesting fact: Wonder's 1980 single, "Happy Birthday" was part of a successful campaign to make civil rights campaigner Martin Luther King Jr.'s birthday into a national holiday.

Wonder believes his lack of sight gave him a heightened awareness of sound.

A Wider Audience

Determined that his message should be heard outside the R&B market, Wonder toured America supporting rock group The Rolling Stones, and recorded with pop artists including Paul McCartney and Elton John.

Wonder has recorded more than 30 United States top 10 hits, and received 22 Grammy Awards. He is still performing today.

Wonder performed in support of Barack Obama at a presidential campaign in Indiana in 2008.

MAKING HISTORY

In 2009, Wonder was named a United Nations Messenger of Peace, having been recognized as "an artist who used his voice and special relationship with the public to defend civil and human rights and to improve the lives of those less fortunate."

Michael Jackson
The King of Pop

Name: Michael Joseph Jackson

Born: August 29, 1958, Gary, Indiana

Died: June 25, 2009

Musical talent: Singing and songwriting

Interesting fact: Jackson was married to Elvis Presley's daughter, Lisa Marie Presley, from 1996 to 1998.

Michael Jackson was born into an African American working-class family, the youngest of five brothers. Their father, Joseph, believed his sons had talent, so he shaped them into a musical group called The Jackson 5. Michael was just five years old when he joined the group!

Chart-Toppers

When the band signed to the famous Motown label in 1968, Joseph Jackson became their manager. He pushed his sons to spend long hours rehearsing. The group went on to have

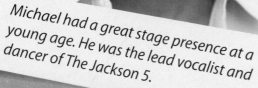

Michael had a great stage presence at a young age. He was the lead vocalist and dancer of The Jackson 5.

many hit singles including "ABC" and "I'll Be There." At the age of 13, Jackson launched his solo career. In 1972, had his first solo number one single, "Ben."

Moving On

The Jackson 5 cut their ties with the Motown label in the mid-1970s and signed a new recording deal with Epic Records. Jackson soon emerged as a talented solo songwriter. Working with legendary producer Quincy Jones, Jackson released his hugely successful 1979 solo album *Off The Wall.*

It was Michael's next solo album, *Thriller* (1982), that made him a legend. The album produced seven top 10 hits and launched Jackson's famous moonwalk dance. The video for the song "Thriller" had stunning special effects. The single stayed in the charts for 80 weeks.

Aid in Africa

Jackson's next two albums *Bad* (1987) and *Dangerous* (1991) were successful, but not on the scale of *Thriller.* During the 1980s and 1990s, Michael worked on several humanitarian projects, including USA for Africa's "We Are The World," which raised funds for aid in Africa.

Final Years

From the early 1990s on, Jackson's private life made the headlines, and by the 2000s his eccentricity began to overshadow his musical talent. Jackson planned a comeback tour for 2009, but he died following a heart attack at his home in Los Angeles. He was 50 years old.

Here, Jackson performs on stage at Wembley Stadium in London, during his Bad tour in 1988.

MAKING HISTORY

Michael Jackson was the best-selling black music artist of all time. He was also regarded as one of the most talented, gifted, and eccentric performers we have ever known. His enormous crossover success in music and dance has led to a generation of musicians who are influenced by him, such as Justin Timberlake.

Jay-Z
Hip-Hop Entrepreneur

Name: Shawn Corey Carter

Born: December 4, 1969, Brooklyn, New York

Musical talent: Rapping

Interesting fact: Jay-Z took his name from the J and Z subway trains that ran through his childhood neighborhood of Bedford-Stuyvesant, Brooklyn.

Jay-Z's performance style is smooth and relies on clever wordplay.

Shawn Corey Carter grew up in a single-parent home in the Marcy Projects, in Brooklyn, New York. Shawn sold drugs as a teenager but turned to rap as his ticket to a better life.

Early Business Venture

Shortly after he released his first self-financed record, called *Reasonable Doubt* in 1996, Jay-Z started the Rock-A-Fella record company with two friends. The single "Ain't No Nigga" from *Reasonable Doubt* catapulted Jay-Z to fame. '

Jay-Z Effect

Before long, Jay-Z had changed rap from a music style that sensationalized violence to a new style of rap that celebrated designer clothing, expensive cars, and flashy jewelry.

Rap Entrepreneur

Jay-Z continued to produce best-selling albums, such as the Grammy Award-winning *Vol.2 Hard Knock Life* (1998) and *The Blueprint 3* (2009), featuring his successful "New York State of Mind," which was number one on the Billboard Hot 100 for five weeks in a row. His interest in the business side of the music industry is what sets him apart from other artists. He is one of the most financially successful rap artists in the world. He has made millions from his business ventures.

In 2008, Jay-Z married Beyoncé, one of the most successful pop artists of all time. Jay-Z is fast becoming a modern music legend.

Beyoncé
The R&B Sensation

The daughter of an African American father and a Creole mother, Beyoncé attended singing, ballet, and jazz dance classes from a very early age.

Forming Destiny's Child

At eight years old, Beyoncé was a member of an all-girl group called Girl's Tyme, which eventually became Destiny's Child. In 1997 the band, managed by Beyoncé's father Matthew, signed to Columbia Records. Destiny's Child went on to sell over 20 million albums, with strong female-centric hits including "Independent Woman Part 1" and "Survivor" (2001).

Going Solo

By 2003, all of the band members had moved on to solo projects and Beyoncé released *Dangerously In Love*. The five-million selling album had two hit singles, including "Crazy In Love," a collaboration with her now-husband, rapper Jay-Z, and started her on the path to phenomenal solo success.

Social Conscience

Beyoncé has long supported social causes. She and her Destiny's Child bandmate Kelly Rowland founded the Survivor Foundation, to provide housing for the victims of 2005's Hurricane Katrina. She also supported World Children's Day and Hope for Haiti in 2010.

To watch Beyoncé live in concert is to be amazed by her energy, dance routines, and spectacular stage shows!

MAKING HISTORY

In 2010, Beyoncé set the record for the most Grammy Awards won in one night, when she won six awards. She is ranked by *Forbes* magazine as the most powerful and influential musician in the world.

Other Music Heroes

Duke Ellington (1899–1974)

This jazz band leader and composer was born in Washington, DC. He wrote his first composition before he had even learned to read music. In 1923, he moved to New York and was a regular performer at the famous jazz venue, the Cotton Club. In 1969, President Richard Nixon threw a party at the White House to celebrate the 70th birthday of this great musical legend.

Nat King Cole (1919–1965)

A jazz pianist, songwriter, and vocalist Cole was taught music by his mother. In 1939, he formed the King Cole Trio and toured Europe, playing in front of the future Queen Elizabeth II. Cole faced racism throughout his career, and eventually stopped playing venues in the segregated South. He made many successful TV appearances before he died of lung cancer at the age of 46.

Jazzie B (1963–)

This DJ, rapper, and songwriter was born in London, United Kingdom. With producer Nellee Hooper, they formed a musical collective called Soul II Soul, which went on to be one of the most innovative dance/R&B outfits of the 1980s. In 2008, he was honored by Great Britain and received the Ivor Novello award for being "the man who gave black British music a soul of its own."

Ella Fitzgerald (1917–1996)

As a 16 year old, jazz singer Fitzgerald won first prize in a singing competition in New York. She joined a band called the Savoy Swing Orchestra and made her first record in 1938. Four years later she launched her solo singing career and went on to become known as "The First Lady of Jazz."

Jimi Hendrix (1942–1970)

This rock guitarist and singer was born in Seattle, Washington. He played the guitar from childhood. In 1966, he went to England and formed a band called The Jimi Hendrix Experience. An exciting performer, Hendrix soon earned a wild reputation. His lifestyle began to cause him problems and he died a drug-related death at the age of 27.

Alicia Keys (1981–)

This R&B and hip hop artist was born in New York City. Her musical talent began to emerge at a very early age, starting with taking piano lessons at the age of five. She began to practice her songwriting skills in her early teens. Her musical influences while growing up were diverse, ranging from rappers Biggie Smalls and Tupac Shakur, to jazz musicians Miles Davis and Nina Simone, to Stevie Wonder.

Timeline

Legacy

1875 Samuel Coleridge-Taylor is born

1901 Louis Armstrong is born

1920s Jazz music reaches its peak of popularity

1928 Paul Robeson shoots to fame appearing in *Show Boat* in London

1933 James Brown is born

1929–1930s The Great Depression begins in 1929 and lasts for more than a decade

1950 Stevie Wonder is born

1956 James Brown's first single "Please, Please, Please" sells 3 million copies

1964 Shirley Bassey's James Bond theme "Goldfinger" becomes a number 1 hit in the United Kingdom and United States

1968 The Jackson 5 signs to the Motown label

1976 Bob Marley flees to London after a failed assassination attempt in Jamaica

1982 Michael Jackson's *Thriller* album becomes the biggest-selling album of all time

2003 Jay-Z and Beyoncé collaborate on the single "Crazy in Love"

2009 Michael Jackson dies

The legacies of the musicians in this book live on, not only in their achievements, but also through the work of their families, friends, and followers:

http://www.thesurvivorfoundation.com/
Beyoncé and former Destiny's Child bandmate Kelly Rowland set up the Survivor Foundation to provide help for victims of disasters, including housing for victims of Hurricane Katrina.

http://www.bobmarley-foundation.com/foundation.html
The Bob Marley Foundation was set up in 1986 and continues to support communities in need across the world.

http://jamesbrownfamilyfdn.org/site
The Brown Family Children Foundation began in 2007 to continue a legacy started by James Brown, who set up projects to help underprivileged children and poor families.

Glossary

activism (AK-tiv-is-um) To take direct action (such as a protest or demonstration) to achieve a goal.

assassination (uh-sas-suh-NAY-shun) To murder a prominent figure.

black consciousness (BLAK KON-shus-nes) A movement seeking to unite black people and take pride in the black race.

blaxploitation (blak-sploy-TAY-shun) The word is a mix of 'black' and 'exploitation'. Films featuring black actors. They were designed to appeal to a black audience.

crossover (KROS-oh-ver) This refers to a black artist who has success appealing to a majority white audience.

discrimination (dis-krih-muh-NAY-shun) The unfair treatment of a group or person, based on their race.

Great Depression (GRAYT dih-PREH-shun) A period during the 1930s when there was a worldwide economic depression.

Mahler (MAH-lur) Gustav Mahler (1860–1911) was a famous Austrian composer and one of the leading conductors of his time.

nationalist (NASH-nul-ist) Somebody who supports the independence of a country or people.

plantation (plan-TAY-shun) A large estate or farm where crops are grown and tended to by workers.

racial integration (RAY-shul in-tuh-GRAY-shun) To join races together.

racism (RAY-sih-zum) Abusive behaviour towards another race.

R&B (R and B) A style of music mixing rhythm and blues.

Rastafari movement (rah-stuh-FAR-ee MOOV-ment) A form of religion that originated in Jamaica and regards Haile Selassie (or Ras Tafari), the former emperor of Ethiopia, as God.

reggae (REH-gay) A style of music, originating in Jamaica.

scatting (SKAT-ing) Jazz singing that uses vocal sounds instead of words.

segregation (seh-grih-GAY-shn) To be set apart from a main group.

ska (SKA) A fast style of music with a strong off beat, which originated in Jamaica.

subversion (sub-VER-zhun) To act against a governing power or authority.

Watergate scandal (WAH-ter-gayt SKAN-dul) A 1970s political scandal in the USA which led to the resignation of the President of the United States, Richard Nixon, on August 9, 1974.

Index